LIGHTNING BOLT BOOKS™

Gray Everywhere

Kristin Sterling

Lerner Publications Company

Minneapolis

To the teachers at Hoover Elementary. Go Gray Wolves!

Lerner Publications Company
A division of Lerner Publishing Group, Inc.
241 First Avenue North
Minneapolis, MN 55401 U.S.A.

Website address: www.lernerbooks.com

Library of Congress Cataloging-in-Publication Data

Sterling, Kristin.
    Gray everywhere / by Kristin Sterling.
        p.   cm. — (Lightning bolt books™—Colors everywhere)
    Includes index.
    ISBN 978-0-7613-5439-0 (lib. bdg. : alk. paper)
    1. Gray—Juvenile literature. I. Title.
    QC495.5.S745 2011
    535.6—dc22   2009038844

Manufactured in the United States of America
1 – BP – 7/15/10

Contents

The Secret Color

Gray is undercover. Gray is secret. Gray is a color that doesn't always get noticed.

The forgotten color is all around.
Gray is everywhere!

All these rocks
are shades of gray.

Gray is found in the wide-open oceans. Gray whales glide through waves with grace.

This gray whale makes bubbles in the water.

Dolphins play and splash like children.

Their smooth gray skin flashes against a blue sky.

Gray can be found in forests. Small gray squirrels hurry to bury their nutty treasures.

Gray wolves move quietly through the woods. The pack is hunting for its next meal.

Look around in a city.
Gray is found here as
well. A small flower pokes
through gray cement.

Gray thunderclouds
gather in the sky.

The smell of rain fills the air.

Gray is found on people of all ages. Some grandmas and grandpas have gray hair.

This grandmother and granddaughter read a book together.

This young woman is wearing a gray silk dress.

13

Shades of Gray

There are many shades of gray.
Some are almost as light as white.
Some are almost as dark as black.

Dove gray is a light, soft color.
Sarah's pet rabbit is dove gray.

Slate gray is a little darker. Kristin types stories on a slate gray computer.

Gray is a common color for computers and keyboards.

Charcoal gray is a deep, dark color. Fluffy and Fifi are charcoal gray kittens.

Black and White Together

Look closely at this black and white photograph. Gray can be found here as well.

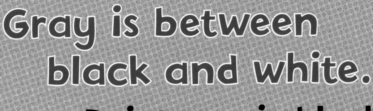

Gray is between black and white.
Painters mix black and white together to make gray.

Try it yourself in a glass bowl. Mix equal parts black and white paint with help from an adult. Which shade did you create?

Try more white than black. Experiment to discover all the shades you can make.

21

Grant Loves Gray

Grant loves the color gray! He thinks it is a calm, beautiful color.

Grant is a photographer.
His favorite photos are
black, white, and gray.

This is Grant's chinchilla. He is soft and loves to snuggle.

Grant has a
light gray bedroom.

It makes him feel comfortable.

Grant's baseball uniform is gray. He is a great player.

What is your favorite color?

Fun Facts

- Gray whales travel more than 12,000 miles (19,000 kilometers) from cold waters near Alaska to warm waters near Mexico every year. They spend winters in the warmer waters and then travel back to cooler waters again.

- Gray kangaroos can hop at speeds more than 35 miles (56 km) an hour! They have very strong hind legs.

- Gray hairstreaks are a type of butterfly. They are gray with brightly colored spots on their wings.

- Most gray wolf packs are also families. Packs usually include a male wolf, a female wolf, and their young pups.

- The human brain is a grayish color. Using your *gray matter* means "using your intelligence."

- Gray elephants are the largest land mammals. They grow as tall as 11 feet (3.4 meters) high and can weigh between 7,000 to 13,000 pounds (3,000 to 6,000 kilograms)!

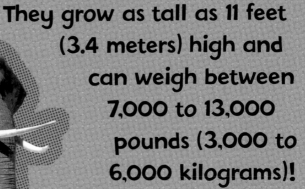

Glossary

chinchilla: a soft, gray rodent

experiment: a test for discovering something

pack: a group of something such as animals, people, or things

shade: the darkness or lightness of a color

treasure: something that is very important or valuable

Further Reading

Brunhoff, Laurent de. *Babar's Book of Color*. New York: Harry N. Abrams, 2004.

Cottin, Menena. *The Black Book of Colors*. Toronto: Groundwood Books, 2008.

Enchanted Learning: Gray
http://www.enchantedlearning.com/colors/gray.shtml

Learn about Color!
http://www.metmuseum.org/explore/Learn_About_Color/index.html

Sterling, Kristin. *Black Everywhere*. Minneapolis: Lerner Publications Company, 2010.

Sterling, Kristin. *White Everywhere*. Minneapolis: Lerner Publications Company, 2010.

Index

Photo Acknowledgments

The images in this book are used with the permission of: © Rozum/Dreamstime.com, p. 1; © Eric Isselée/Shutterstock Images, pp. 2, 29 (bottom), 30; © Loskutnikov/Shutterstock Images, p. 4; © Photobank/Shutterstock Images, p. 5; © Mark Carwardine/Visuals Unlimited, Inc., p. 6; © blickwinkel/Schmidbauer/Alamy, p. 7; © Frank Schneidermeyer/Oxford Scientific/Photolibrary/Getty Images, p. 8; © Jim and Jaimie Dutcher/National Geographic/Getty Images, p. 9; © Elena Kalistratova/Shutterstock Images, p. 10; © Ed Freeman/Stone/Getty Images, p. 11; © Monkey Business Images/Shutterstock Images, p. 12; © Alena Ozerova/Shutterstock Images, p. 13; © Antoine Juliette/Oredia/Alamy, p. 14; © Mike Brinson/The Image Bank/Getty Images, p. 15; © Gualberto Becerra/Shutterstock Images, p. 16; © Dorling Kindersley/Getty Images, p. 17; © Kai Kirkkonen/Gorilla Creative Images/Getty Images, p. 18; © Jamie Grill/Iconica/Getty Images, p. 19; © Todd Strand/Independent Picture Service, pp. 20, 21; © kihoto/iStockphoto.com, pp. 22, 23; © Gala/Kan/Shutterstock Images, p. 24; © Zastol'skiy Victor Leonidovich/Shutterstock Images, p. 25; © Jeff Skopin/Shutterstock Images, p. 26; © Paul Viant/Taxi/Getty Images, p. 27; © Theo Allofs/Photonica/Getty Images, p. 28; © altrendo nature/Getty Images, p. 29 (top); © iofoto/Shutterstock Images, p. 31.

Front cover: © Car Culture/Getty Images (car); © Eric Isselée/Shutterstock Images (kitten); U.S. Navy photo by Rusty Baker (jet); © Photobank/Shutterstock Images (stones); © Four Oaks/Shutterstock Images (elephant); © Peter Sykes/Alamy (statue); © Todd Strand/Independent Picture Service (paint strips).